W9-DET-315

Thanksgiving

by Mari C. Schuh

Consulting Editor: Gail Saunders-Smith, Ph.D.
Consultant: Alexa Sandmann, Ed.D.
Professor of Literacy
The University of Toledo
Member, National Council for the Social Studies

Pebble Books

an imprint of Capstone Press
Mankato, Minnesota

Pebble Books are published by Capstone Press
151 Good Counsel Drive, P.O. Box 669, Mankato, Minnesota 56002
http://www.capstone-press.com

Library of Congress Cataloging-in-Publication Data
Schuh, Mari C., 1975–
    Thanksgiving / by Mari C. Schuh.
    p. cm.—(Holidays and celebrations)
    Includes bibliographical references and index.
    ISBN 0-7368-0981-3
    1. Thanksgiving Day—Juvenile literature. [1. Thanksgiving Day.
2. Holidays.] I. Title. II. Series.
GT4975 .S38 2002
394.2649—dc21   00-012797

Summary: Simple text and photographs describe the history of Thanksgiving and the
ways it is celebrated.

Note to Parents and Teachers

The series Holidays and Celebrations supports national social
studies standards related to culture. This book describes
Thanksgiving and illustrates how it is celebrated. The photographs
support early readers in understanding the text. The repetition of
words and phrases helps early readers learn new words. This book
also introduces early readers to subject-specific vocabulary words,
which are defined in the Words to Know section. Early readers may
need assistance to read some words and to use the Table of
Contents, Words to Know, Read More, Internet Sites, and
Index/Word List sections of the book.

Table of Contents

4

Thanksgiving is a national holiday. People give thanks for their blessings on Thanksgiving.

American Indians and the Pilgrims started the Thanksgiving tradition in America. The Pilgrims came to America from England in 1620. They wanted to start new lives in a new land.

8

American Indians helped the Pilgrims settle in America. The Indians showed the Pilgrims where to hunt and fish. The Indians showed the Pilgrims how to grow different crops.

The Pilgrims had a big harvest in 1621. They were thankful. The Pilgrims and Indians gathered for a feast. This feast was the first Thanksgiving the Pilgrims celebrated in America.

November

S	M	T	W	T	F	S
					1	2
3	4	5	6	7	8	9
10	11	12	13	14	15	16
17	18	19	20	21	22	23
24	25	26	27	28	29	30

12

President Abraham Lincoln
made Thanksgiving a
national holiday in 1863.
Americans celebrate
Thanksgiving every year
on the fourth Thursday
of November.

Some people decorate their homes for Thanksgiving. They use pumpkins, gourds, and corn.

Students learn about
Thanksgiving in school.
They write about why they
are thankful.

Families and friends gather to celebrate Thanksgiving. Some people go to parades or football games.

Turkey, stuffing, and pumpkin pie are Thanksgiving foods. Families and friends often eat this special Thanksgiving meal together.

Words to Know

celebrate—to do something fun on a special occasion

crop—a plant grown in large amounts; most crops are food.

decorate—to add items to make something look nice

feast—a large meal for a lot of people; people have feasts on special occasions.

gourd—a fruit with a rounded shape like a squash or pumpkin

harvest—to gather crops

national—having to do with a country as a whole; Thanksgiving is a national holiday in the United States.

tradition—a custom, idea, or belief that is passed from one generation to the next

Read More

Klingel, Cynthia, and Robert B. Noyed. *Thanksgiving.* Wonder Books. Chanhassen, Minn.: Child's World, 2001.

Rau, Dana Meachen. *Thanksgiving.* A True Book. New York: Children's Press, 2000.

Winne, Joanne. *Let's Get Ready for Thanksgiving.* Celebrations. New York: Children's Press, 2001.

Internet Sites

An American Thanksgiving for Kids and Families
http://www.night.net/thanksgiving

Happy Thanksgiving
http://www.theholidayspot.com/thanksgiving

Thanksgiving Puzzles and Coloring Sheets
http://familyeducation.com/printables/
package/0,2358,1-10681,00.html

Thanksgiving Traditions and History
http://wilstar.com/holidays/thanksgv.htm

Index/Word List

America, 7, 9, 11
American Indians, 7, 9, 11
Americans, 13
blessings, 5
celebrate, 11, 13, 19
decorate, 15
England, 7
families, 19, 21

feast, 11
fish, 9
foods, 21
friends, 19, 21
harvest, 11
holiday, 5, 13
hunt, 9
land, 7
learn, 17
Lincoln, Abraham, 13
national, 5, 13

November, 13
parades, 19
people, 5, 15, 19
Pilgrims, 7, 9, 11
pumpkin pie, 21
school, 17
students, 17
thankful, 11, 17
tradition, 7
turkey, 21

Word Count: 181
Early-Intervention Level: 16

Credits

Heather Kindseth, cover designer; Kia Bielke, production designer; Kimberly Danger, and Deirdre Barton, photo researchers

Bob Daemmrich/Pictor, 4
Capstone Press/Gary Sundermeyer, cover, 14, 16
Culver Pictures/PictureQuest, 8
Index Stock Imagery/David Burch, 1
Library of Congress, 12
North Wind Picture Archives, 6
Photo Network/Tom McCarthy, 20
Photri-Microstock, 10
Unicorn Stock Photos/A. Rameu, 18